LEARN ABOUT
WEATHER

ROBIN KERROD

LORENZ BOOKS
NEW YORK • LONDON • SYDNEY • BATH

First published in 1997 by Lorenz Books

Lorenz Books is an imprint of
Anness Publishing Inc.
27 West 20th Street
New York, New York 10011

ISBN 1 85967 189 6

Publisher: Joanna Lorenz
Senior Editors: Sue Grabham and Caroline Beattie
Editor: Sam Batra
Photographer: John Freeman
Stylist: Thomasina Smith
Designer: Caroline Reeves
Picture Researcher: Liz Eddison
Illustrator: Michael Lamb

Printed in China
Star Standard Industries Pte Ltd.

The Publishers would like to thank the following pupils from St. John the Baptist
Church of England School and Walnut Tree Walk Primary School: Maria
Bloodworth, Tony Borg, Steven Briggs, Jackie Ishiekwene, Daniel Johnson, Jon
Leaning, Erin Macarthy, Hanife Manur, Tanya Martin, Lola Olayinka, and Ini Usoro.
Thanks to West Meters Ltd. for the loan of props.

WEATHER

CONTENTS

4 • Watching weather

6 • The sun's energy

8 • Measuring temperature

10 • The atmosphere

12 • Air and sky

14 • In the air

16 • Features of weather

18 • Air pressure

20 • Air on the move

22 • Measuring the wind

24 • Stormy weather

26 • The water cycle

28 • Humidity

30 • Looking at clouds

32 • Rain and dew

34 • Making rainbows

36 • Thunder and lightning

38 • Gauging the rain

40 • Snow and ice

42 • Masses of air

44 • Holding the heat

46 • World weather

48 • Warm climates

50 • Cool climates

52 • Seasonal weather

54 • Charging up

56 • The changing climate

58 • Recording the weather

60 • Your weather station

62 • Forecasting

64 • Index

WATCHING WEATHER

THE weather affects us all. If it is warm and sunny, we like to spend time outside and wear light clothes. If it is cold and wet, we prefer to stay indoors. If we do go out, it is best to dress in layers and carry an umbrella. What exactly does the word weather mean? It means the conditions in the air around us – how hot it is, how strong the wind is, whether it is sunny or cloudy, whether it is dry or wet. As the weather is so important, thousands of scientists around the world study it. The scientific study of the weather is called meteorology, and the scientists who study it are called meteorologists. One of their main jobs is to forecast the weather, that is, tell us what the weather is going to be like in the future. However, their forecasts are not always right!

It is winter and the weather forecast says it is going to be cold and wet. You need to put on warm, waterproof clothes. Remember an umbrella!

Snowball fights are a lot of fun as long as the snowballs miss you. Snow is fun to play in, but it can make traveling very dangerous.

In the summer, the sun is so strong that you need to wear a hat and sunglasses. The coolest place to be is in the water, but even there you need protection. Anyone for a swim?

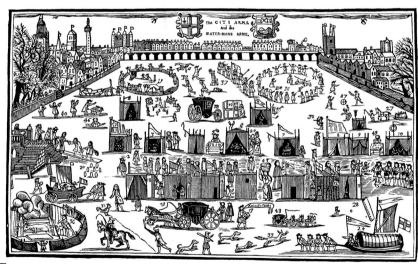

Learning about the sun

Floating high above the earth in space, a satellite called *Solar Max* keeps a close eye on the sun. The results it sends back help scientists to understand how the sun affects the world's weather and climate.

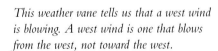

This weather vane tells us that a west wind is blowing. A west wind is one that blows from the west, not toward the west.

Frozen over

Changes in the sun's heat output could have caused the Little Ice Age that occurred in the 1600s. During this time, the Thames froze so hard in London's winters that Frost Fairs could be held on it. The picture above shows the Frost Fair of 1683.

THE SUN'S ENERGY

THE earth gets almost all of its heat from the sun. The sun is a star. Like other stars, it releases tremendous amounts of heat, light and other forms of energy into space. Only a small amount of the sun's energy reaches the earth, but it is enough to power our weather systems. Its energy can make rocks so hot that you can fry eggs on them. It can create tornadoes that toss cars high into the air. Varying amounts of the sun's heat fall on different parts of the world. That is the main reason why places around the world have different weather. The amount of heat a place receives from the sun also changes with the seasons.

Core

Energy flow

The sun's energy is produced in the center, or the core. There, the temperature reaches about 27,000,000 degrees Fahrenheit. At this temperature, atoms of gas fuse, or combine together, and give out enormous amounts of energy. This energy escapes into space, mainly as light and heat.

Heating the earth

The sun pours energy onto the earth. Some of it bounces off the atmosphere back into space. Some heats up the air, but most heats up the ground and the oceans.

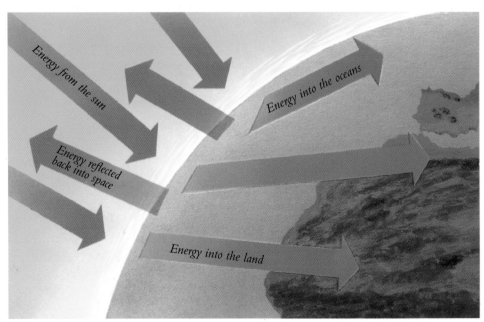

Energy from the sun

Energy into the oceans

Energy reflected back into space

Energy into the land

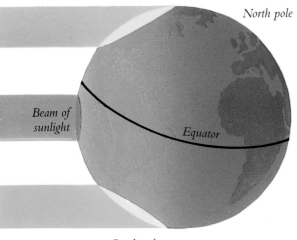

North pole

Beam of
sunlight

Equator

South pole

Sunlight into electricity

Solar power plants capture the sun's energy and turn it into electricity. This huge plant in California uses hundreds of mirrors to reflect sunlight onto a boiler at the top of the tower.

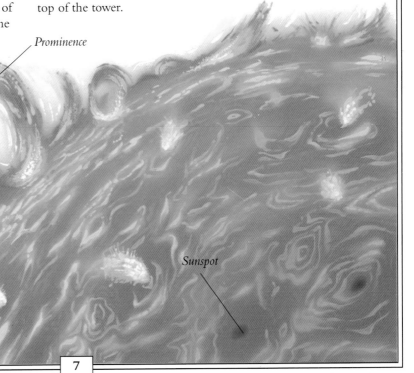

Prominence

Sunspot

Cooler or warmer?

The sun's energy does not fall evenly over the earth because the earth is round. Imagine three beams of sunlight (*above*) of the same size and with the same energy falling on the earth. One falls on the equator and the others on the north and south poles. As the beam falling on the equator covers a much smaller area, its energy is more concentrated and the temperature is higher.

The surface of the sun is a stormy sea of bubbling, boiling gases. In some places, great fountains of gas, called prominences, shoot high above the surface. The temperature of most of the surface is about 10,000 degrees Fahrenheit. Dark patches, called sunspots, are cooler.

MEASURING TEMPERATURE

WHAT we notice most about the weather is the temperature – how hot or how cold it is. We measure the temperature with a thermometer, a word that literally means heat measurer. Ordinary thermometers have a column of liquid in a glass tube. When the temperature goes up, the liquid expands and the column of liquid gets longer. The amount the column lengthens is a measure of how much the temperature has increased. This means that thermometers can be used to show a broad range of temperatures. The liquids used most in thermometers are mercury and alcohol. They are used because they do not boil or freeze at temperatures we find in the home. But we can make a simple thermometer using water.

This wall thermometer is filled with alcohol colored blue. It has two temperature scales: degrees Celsius (°C) and degrees Fahrenheit (°F).

Thermo-strips
You can take your temperature by pressing a thermo-strip against your forehead. The strip that shows your temperature changes color. The strip *(above)* indicates 103 degrees Fahrenheit, but usually it registers 98-99 degrees Fahrenheit, which is the normal body temperature for human beings.

FACT BOX

• A pleasant room temperature for human beings is 75 degrees Fahrenheit.

• In 1922, at a place called Al´Aziziyah, in Libya, the temperature in the shade rose to 140 degrees Fahrenheit.

• Water freezes into ice when the temperature falls to 32 degrees Fahrenheit.

• In parts of North America and northern Europe, temperatures can fall to more than minus 40 degrees Fahrenheit in winter.

• At a temperature of about 374 degrees Fahrenheit below freezing, the air we breathe turns into liquid.

MATERIALS

You will need: pitcher of water, bottle, food coloring, clear straw, reusable adhesive, piece of cardboard, scissors, felt-tip marker.

Make a thermometer

1 Pour cold water into the bottle until it is about two-thirds full. Add some coloring. Dip the straw into the water and seal the neck tightly with reusable adhesive.

2 Blow into the straw to force extra air into the bottle. After a few seconds, the extra air pressure inside will force the water level to rise up the straw.

3 Cut the cardboard and slot it over the straw, as in the picture. Let the bottle stand for a while. Make a mark on the cardboard by the water level to show room temperature. Now your thermometer is ready to take outside into the sunlight—that is, if the sun is shining!

4 The sun's heat will make the air and water in the bottle expand. This will force the water level in the straw above the room temperature mark. Now put your thermometer in the refrigerator for two hours. What do you notice? The water level in the tube will drop below the room temperature mark. Make a note of it on your thermometer.

THE ATMOSPHERE

THE air around us forms a layer that covers the earth. We call this layer the atmosphere. The atmosphere is most dense, or thickest, near the ground. It gets less dense, or thinner, the higher up you go. At a height of about 186 miles there is scarcely any air left at all. This is the beginning of space. Most of our weather takes place in the lowest and thickest part of the atmosphere, in a layer that we call the troposphere. This layer is between 6 and 10 miles thick. It is in this layer that clouds form, rain and snow fall, and thunder and lightning take place. In the next part of the atmosphere, called the stratosphere, there is a layer of a gas called ozone. This is very important to us because it blocks dangerous rays coming from the sun.

Working in space above the atmosphere, astronauts must wear spacesuits to survive. The suit supplies them with oxygen to breathe and also protects them from the sun's heat.

Space
The edge of the atmosphere is only about a hundred miles above the earth, then space begins. Above the atmosphere is the moon, nearly 238,700 miles away.

Heavenly bodies

The thin streak *(above)* was made by a meteor, or shooting star. This is a small piece of rock that burns up when it plunges into the atmosphere. The broader trail was made by a comet, which is a huge lump of icy rock that gradually breaks up in space. Occasionally we can see comets in the sky.

Lights in the sky

Strange glowing patches appear in the skies above Alaska. They can also be seen in areas around the north and south poles. In the north, as in Alaska, they are called the Northern Lights, or the Aurora Borealis. In the south they are called the Southern Lights, or the Aurora Australis.

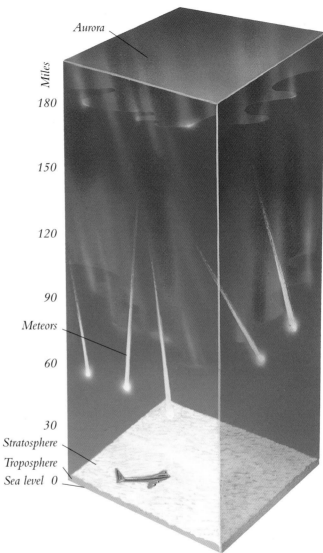

Miles

Aurora

180

150

120

90

Meteors

60

30

Stratosphere

Troposphere

Sea level 0

A section of the earth's atmosphere showing the different layers that make it up.

11

AIR AND SKY

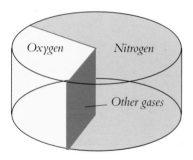

THE air that makes up the atmosphere is a gas that we cannot see, feel, taste or smell. Actually, it is not one gas, but a mixture of many different gases. The two main gases are called nitrogen and oxygen. The pie chart below shows you that there is nearly four times as much nitrogen as oxygen. However, to living things, oxygen is the most important gas. Almost all living things must breathe in oxygen to stay alive. The air also contains small amounts of other gases. One of these is carbon dioxide. Plants take in this gas to make their food, and animals give off this gas when they exhale. Much of the carbon dioxide in the air comes from cars and factories that burn fuels such as oil and coal.

Paragliding is a seaside sport. Wearing a parachute, you get towed high into the air behind a boat and then float down to the ground.

This pie chart shows the amounts of the main gases that make up the air.

Blue sky
The sky looks blue because the air particles scatter more blue light into our eyes than any other color.

Plants and animals

Plants and animals affect the air in different ways. Plants take in carbon dioxide from the air and give off oxygen. Animals do the opposite. They take in oxygen from the air and give off carbon dioxide.

Carried in the air

The air contains minute traces of many different substances, such as the scent and pollen of flowers.

Red sky

In the evening, the sky often turns orange or red. This happens because dust in the lower air blocks the blue rays in the sunlight when the sun is low. Only orange and red rays are able to pass through.

Oxygen for life

Like all animals, we get our energy by burning food inside our bodies. We take in the oxygen to burn our food when we breathe air into our lungs.

IN THE AIR

As we have seen, air is made up of a mixture of different gases, mainly nitrogen and oxygen. We can find out roughly how much oxygen there is in the air with this simple experiment. The oxygen from the air can be removed in a jar by burning a candle in it. When things burn, they combine with oxygen. During the experiment, water rises in the jar to take the place of the oxygen. By noting how much the water rises, you can easily figure out how much oxygen was in the jar to start with. You should find that the water level rises by about one-fifth of the height of the jar.

These balloons are filled with a gas that is lighter than air. If you let go of their strings, they will float away into heavier air.

M A T E R I A L S

You will need: candle, clear mixing bowl, reusable adhesive, pitcher with colored water, glass jar, felt-tip marker.

Measure the oxygen

1 Stick the candle on the bottom of the bowl with reusable adhesive. Pour the water into the bowl up to 2 inches deep.

2 Ask an adult to light the candle and then place the jar over it. Let the jar rest on the bottom of the bowl and watch what happens.

3 The water rises until the candle goes out. Mark the water level on the jar, as this will show how much oxygen was present initially.

See the weight

We cannot see the air around us and cannot usually feel it. In fact, we almost forget it is there most of the time. Air seems weightless, but air has weight just like any other material. A large balloon is heavier than a small one because it contains more air, as this experiment shows.

M A T E R I A L S

You will need: tape, ruler, thread, 2 balloons of equal size, balloon pump.

1 Stick a piece of tape onto the middle of the ruler. Tie a piece of thread around the tape and hold up the ruler.

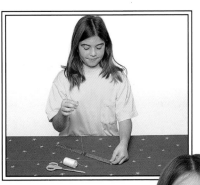

2 Lifting the ruler, adjust the position of the thread so that the ruler balances.

3 Blow up one balloon a little and the other much more. Stick them to opposite ends of the ruler.

4 Hold up the ruler with the thread and see what happens. The large balloon makes the ruler dip down. It is heavier than the small balloon because it contains more air.

FEATURES OF WEATHER

THE three main things that help us to describe the weather are temperature, humidity and pressure. The humidity tells us how much moisture there is in the air. Pressure is the pressure of the atmosphere. It is called the atmospheric pressure. The atmosphere has weight and presses down on the ground with a certain force. In fact, at sea level it presses down on each square ½ inch of surface with a force of about 2.2 pounds. In practice, the pressure varies a little from place to place across the earth. These differences in pressure cause the air to move around. Air moves from a region of high pressure to one of lower pressure, often bringing about changes in the temperature and humidity.

Joshua trees in the deserts of southern California. It is very hot there, and hardly any rain falls during the year. Only a few kinds of plants can survive the drought conditions by storing water.

Hot and wet
These are the Everglades in Florida. It's very hot there, but plenty of rain falls during the year. The Everglades National Park is a huge shallow river where hundreds of different plants and animals thrive. These include alligators in the swampy areas.

FACT BOX

• When you hold out your hand, palm upward, you are supporting a weight of about 2.2 pounds. This is the weight of the air pressing down on your hand.

• The least humid, or driest, places on earth are the hot deserts. The most humid places are the tropical rainforests near the equator.

• When the weather is hot and humid, our skin feels sticky. This happens because when it is hot, we perspire – our skin gives off tiny drops of water. Normally the water quickly evaporates, or vanishes, into the air. But when the weather is humid, the water stays on the skin much longer.

Coldest
The coldest place on earth is Antarctica. The world's lowest temperature was recorded there in July 1983. It was minus 89.2 degrees Celsius.

Air pressure
When you pump up the tires on your bike, you increase the pressure of the air in them. Increased air pressure makes air masses move around the world.

Hottest
The hottest place on earth is Death Valley in California. Daily summer temperatures may stay above 120 degrees Fahrenheit for over a month.

AIR PRESSURE

WHENEVER one thing presses against another, it exerts pressure. Pressure is a kind of force. A heavy book resting on a table exerts pressure on the part of the table underneath it. Air may not be heavy like a book, but it still exerts pressure. It presses down on everything around us including human bodies, although we cannot feel it. We cannot feel it because the pressure inside our bodies equals the air pressure outside, so the two cancel each other out. Differences in the pressure of the air in different places causes the air to move around as the wind. Here we show you some tricks that involve the pressure of the air. We can use air pressure to knock down some books. Air pressure also helps to show that sometimes paper appears to be stronger than wood, as air pressure can hold it in place. In a fizzy experiment, other gases, besides air, exert pressure.

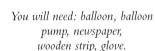

You will need: balloon, balloon pump, newspaper, wooden strip, glove.

Knocking over books
Place a balloon under some books and blow air into it with a balloon pump. As you pump, the air pressure inside the balloon rises. The increased force on the books pushes the pile over.

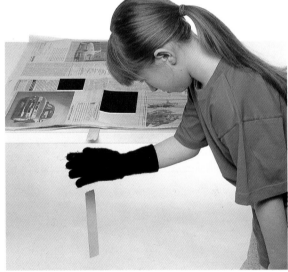

Chopping wood
Cover the wooden strip with newspaper on a table. Leave one third of the wood overhanging. Wear a glove and strike that part. It breaks, but the paper does not.

Create air pressure

You will need: funnel, bottle, vinegar, balloon, baking powder.

1 Place the funnel in the neck of the bottle and pour in some vinegar, about halfway up.

2 Place the funnel in the neck of the balloon. Carefully trickle some baking powder into it.

3 Fit the neck of the balloon carefully over the neck of the bottle, letting the powder-filled part hang down. Gently turn the main body of the balloon over.

4 Let the baking powder fall into the vinegar. The balloon blows up as the mixture starts to fizz.

5 The fizzing shows that a chemical reaction is taking place between the vinegar and the baking powder. This reaction makes lots of gas. As more gas is produced, its pressure rises. The rising gas pressure forces the balloon to expand.

AIR ON THE MOVE

Flying a kite is easy, but only when there is a breeze that is not too strong.

We do not usually notice the air until it moves. Moving air is called wind. Winds blow from regions of high pressure to regions of low pressure. Gentle winds are called breezes. These almost always blow at the seaside. They occur because of the difference in temperature between the sea and the land. This sets up differences in pressure, and it is what causes the breezes. The speed of the wind varies greatly. A breeze is a wind with a speed of up to 30 miles per hour. Gales are stronger winds that travel up to 60 miles per hour. Storm winds travel at speeds of 75 miles per hour. Winds stronger than this are called hurricanes. They can cause great damage and destruction to anything they come across. Hurricanes are greatly feared in those parts of the world where they occur.

WIND FORCE

The force, or strength, of the wind varies widely. A scale called the Beaufort Scale is used to describe the force of the wind. The scale goes from Force 0, which means the air is calm, to Force 12, which means a hurricane is blowing. One way you can guess the force of the wind is by the effect it has on you.

When the wind is Force 0, you cannot feel it. Smoke from chimneys goes straight up. When the wind has reached Force 2, you can feel it on your face and it is called a breeze.

You can feel a Force 4 breeze pushing against your body when you walk.

| 0 | 1 | 2 | 3 | 4 | 5 |

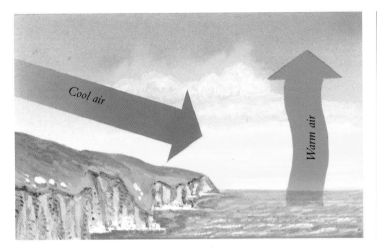

Land breezes and sea breezes

A breeze always blows at the seaside. At night, the land becomes cooler than the sea. Warm air rises above the sea, pulling in cool air from the land as a land breeze. The opposite happens during the day, when a sea breeze blows in from the sea.

Wind power

Giant propellers harness the power of the wind at a wind farm. This one is at Altamont Pass in California. The propellers drive turbines that produce electricity for homes.

At Force 7, the wind has become a gale. You have to bend your body to walk against it.

At Force 9, the wind blows at 50 miles per hour or more. You have to squat down, otherwise you will be blown over.

As the wind increases to Forces 10 and 11, you have to stay flat on the ground to stop yourself from being blown away. Do not go out in a Force 12 hurricane, or it will take you with it!

| 6 | 7 | 8 | 9 | 10 | 11 | 12 |

MEASURING THE WIND

THE wind plays a very important part in meteorology (the study of weather and climate). It shifts the air from place to place and brings about changes in the weather. Meteorologists measure the direction of the wind to help them forecast where the changes will take place. They also measure the speed of the wind to give them an accurate weather prediction. To measure the wind direction, they use an instrument called a weather vane. Learn how to make a simple one here.

The harder you blow on your windmills, the faster they spin around.

M A T E R I A L S

You will need: reusable adhesive, plastic container with lid, scissors, garden stick, plastic straws, colored cardboard, pen, tape, pin, compass, plywood.

Make a weather vane

1 Stick a ball of reusable adhesive to the middle of the lid of the container. Ask an adult to pierce a hole in the bottom of the container with scissors. Put it on the lid.

2 Slide a piece of garden stick into a straw and trim the stick so that it is a bit shorter than the straw. Push the straw and stick through the pot's hole into the reusable adhesive.

3 Cut out a square of cardboard and mark each corner with a point of the compass – N, S, E, W. Snip a hole in the middle and slip it carefully over the straw.

In a spin

Your windmill will give you an idea of how fast the wind is blowing. The faster the wind blows, the faster the windmill will spin.

Windy ways

When you have made your weather vane, take it outside. Use a compass to turn the compass cardboard so that the corners point in the right directions. Now let the wind blow!

4 Cut out two triangles from cardboard and stick them to each end of a straw to form an arrow head and tail. Put a plug of reusable adhesive in the top of the straw.

5 Put a pin through the middle of the arrow and stick it into the reusable adhesive in the straw. Be careful when using sharp objects such as pins.

6 Secure your weather vane with some reusable adhesive on the plywood. Test it for use – the arrow should spin around freely when the wind blows on it.

STORMY WEATHER

WHEN the weather is very rough and windy, we say it is stormy. But, strictly speaking, a storm is the name for a particular kind of strong wind. Sometimes, on hot, dusty days in summer, little dust storms spring up. They are called dust devils. These little whirling winds pick up the dust, but do not do any harm. Some whirlwinds, however, such as tornadoes, are very destructive. They are great funnels of wind, in which the wind rushes around at speeds of up to 300 miles per hour. They form over the land. Hurricanes, which form over the sea, are much larger. They can measure more than 300 miles across.

A spiraling column of wind picks up the dust, creating a dust devil. Dust devils often form over hot, dry farmland in summer.

Spiral of wind
This is what a hurricane looks like from space. The clouds form in a great spiral, getting thicker toward the center. Down below on the ground, the winds reach speeds approaching 125 miles per hour.

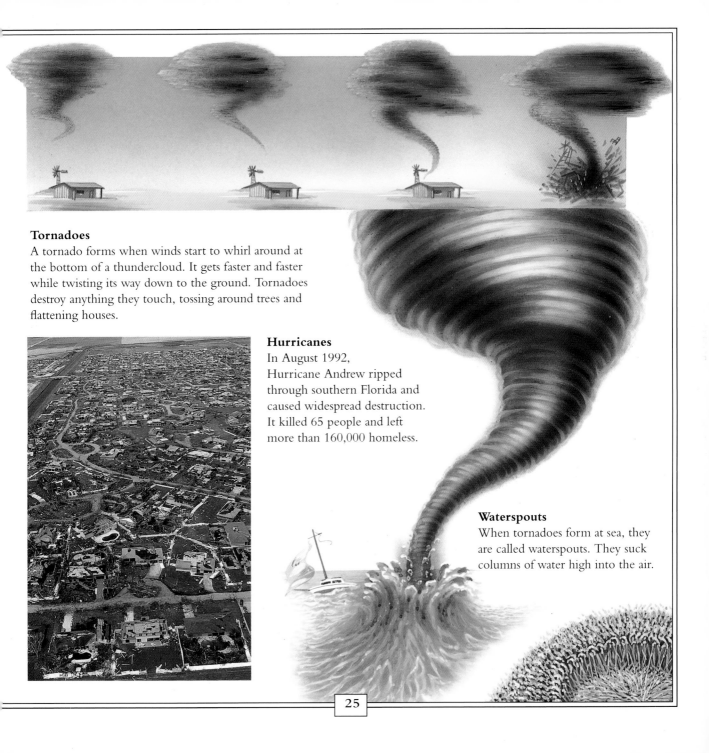

Tornadoes

A tornado forms when winds start to whirl around at the bottom of a thundercloud. It gets faster and faster while twisting its way down to the ground. Tornadoes destroy anything they touch, tossing around trees and flattening houses.

Hurricanes

In August 1992, Hurricane Andrew ripped through southern Florida and caused widespread destruction. It killed 65 people and left more than 160,000 homeless.

Waterspouts

When tornadoes form at sea, they are called waterspouts. They suck columns of water high into the air.

THE WATER CYCLE

THE amount of moisture, or water, there is in the air has a great effect on the weather. For example, if there is a lot of water the chances are that it will rain. On the other hand, if the air is dry it should be clear. The amount of moisture in the air is called the humidity. Water is usually found in the air as a gas called water vapor. The water vapor gets into the air mainly from the oceans, lakes and rivers. It is produced when the heat from the sun warms up surface water and makes it evaporate, or turn to gas. The water vapor rises into the air. The air is cooler higher up. The vapor cools so much that it condenses, or changes back into tiny droplets of liquid water. The droplets gather together to form the great billowing masses that we call clouds. Often they grow bigger and bigger until they become heavy enough to fall from the clouds, as rain – or snow, if it is cold enough. This movement of water from the ground to the air and back again occurs continually and is called the water cycle.

Rain falls

Melted snow from mountains

Water evaporates from lakes

Water evaporates from trees

Water flows into rivers

26

Water vapor turns into droplets and forms clouds

The sun provides the energy that powers the water cycle. It pours heat onto the earth, which makes water evaporate from the rivers and the seas. The water vapor rises into the sky, where it cools and turns into droplets of liquid water.

Water evaporates from sea

In a cloud

High up on Mount Tasman in New Zealand, you might find yourself in a cloud. This is because higher up a mountain, the air becomes cooler. When it is cool enough, clouds form. You can feel how damp the air becomes.

HUMIDITY

THERE is always a certain amount of water in the air, in the form of a gas called water vapor. Meteorologists call the amount of water vapor in the air the humidity. When there is a lot of water vapor around, the air feels humid, or sticky. When there is little water vapor around, the air feels dry. Measuring the amount of water vapor in the air helps meteorologists with their forecasts. When the air gets very humid, for example, the chances are that it will soon rain. An instrument called a hygrometer is used to measure humidity. Learn how to make a simple one here.

You will need: 2 sheets of colored cardboard, scissors, pen, glue, toothpick, straw, reusable adhesive, used matchstick, blotting paper, hole punch.

In the rainforests along the coast of northern California, it stays warm and humid most of the time. In this climate the redwood trees there can grow more than 100 yards tall.

Measure the humidity

1 Cut a piece of cardboard into a rectangle. Mark along one side at regular intervals for a scale. Make a cut about 1 inch long in the bottom. Cut the parts out. Glue them to another piece of cardboard.

2 The second piece of cardboard forms the base. Cut another long rectangle from the first piece of cardboard. Fold and stick to the base as shown above. Pierce top carefully with a toothpick to form a pivot.

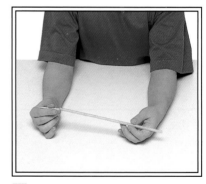

3 Make a pointer using a straw. Attach the used matchstick to one end with some reusable adhesive to hold it firmly in place. This way the pointer has some weight and is not easily knocked off balance.

Transpiring plants

Plants play an important part in the water cycle because their leaves give off water vapor. This is called transpiration. Cover a potted plant with a clear plastic bag, sealing it around the pot with tape. Place the plant in the sunlight for two hours. Notice that the bag starts to mist up and droplets of water form on the inside. They form when the water vapor given off by the plant condenses, or turns back to liquid.

4 Cut several squares of blotting paper and punch a hole in the middle of each one. Slide the squares over the end of the pointer.

5 Now pierce the pointer with the pivot and position the pointer as shown above. Make sure it can swing freely up and down.

6 Your hygrometer is now ready for use. Adjust the position of the toothpick so that the pointer is horizontal. Take your hygrometer into the bathroom when you take a bath. The high humidity in the bathroom should make the blotting paper damp. It will tip the pointer up. Outside, on a warm day, the blotting paper will dry and the pointer will tip down.

LOOKING AT CLOUDS

Cloud of ice crystals

Cloud of water droplets

Water vapor rises

CLOUDS are great fluffy masses of tiny water droplets or ice crystals hanging in the sky. The kinds of clouds we see reveal much about the weather. There are three main kinds of clouds. The most familiar kind is the cumulus. This is the fluffy cloud of fine summer days, looking like a ball of cotton wool. A stratus cloud, on the other hand, is flat and can stretch all across the sky. It brings dull weather and often rain. The stratus is a low cloud. The third main kind of cloud – cirrus – is a very high cloud that can form up to 8 miles up in the air. The cirrus is a wispy, feathery kind of cloud, made up of ice crystals rather than water droplets. Dark clouds that bring rain are called nimbus. Cloud names can be combined. For example, a cumulonimbus cloud is a dark cumulus cloud that brings heavy rain.

Clouds form when warm air containing water vapor rises into the air and cools. The vapor turns into droplets of water, forming clouds. If the air is very cold, the vapor turns into a cloud of tiny ice crystals.

Cumulus
These unusual cumulus clouds look rather like teeth. They are lit dramatically by a low evening Sun.

Cirrus
A fine cirrus cloud formation. You can see why this type of cloud is often called mares' tails.

Cumulonimbus
This great cumulus cloud is expanding into a thunder cloud and will soon develop into the anvil shape of a cumulonimbus.

Cirrocumulus
A classic mackerel sky, so called because it looks a lot like the pattern on the back of the common sea fish, the mackerel. These clouds are called cirrocumulus.

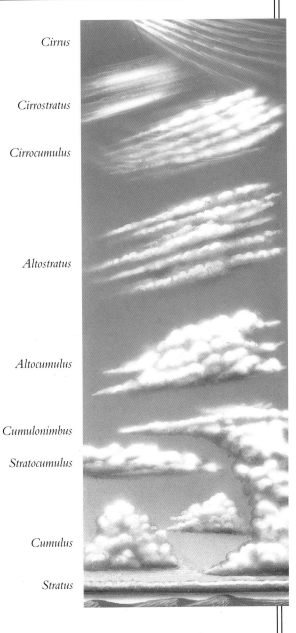

Cirrus

Cirrostratus

Cirrocumulus

Altostratus

Altocumulus

Cumulonimbus

Stratocumulus

Cumulus

Stratus

The main kinds of clouds we see in the sky.

RAIN AND DEW

In some clouds the tiny water droplets remain tiny and stay up in the air. In others the droplets keep bumping into one another and joining together. They get larger and larger, eventually becoming heavy enough to fall out of the cloud as rain. On average, raindrops measure only about 1⁄10 inch across. But the drops that fall from thunderclouds are much bigger. Rain is the commonest form of what meteorologists call precipitation, or something that comes out of the air and falls to the ground. Dew is another kind of precipitation. It forms on the ground and other surfaces on cool nights. The cool surfaces make the water vapor in the air condense into droplets of liquid water.

It can be fun going out in the rain, if you are dressed properly. But watch that umbrella if the wind is strong. It may turn inside out, or carry you away!

Rain to come
Stormy weather off the island of Majorca in the Mediterranean Sea. The dark nimbus clouds are piling up. The sun seems to be drawing water from the sea. Soon it will be raining hard.

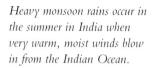

Heavy monsoon rains occur in the summer in India when very warm, moist winds blow in from the Indian Ocean.

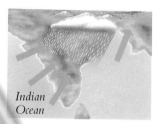

Indian
Ocean

Rainbows

When it is raining and the sun is low in the sky, you can often see a rainbow. This beautiful band of colors is produced when sunlight passes through raindrops.

Lots of rain

The monsoon rain falls in Jaipur, India. In a few months, 30 feet of rain may fall. The rest of the year is parched and dry.

Moist air

In hot, tropical regions such as Hawaii, rain falls regularly throughout the year. The heat and humidity, or moisture, provide perfect growing conditions for all kinds of plants.

Dew drops glisten on the delicate strands of a spider's web in the early morning.

MAKING RAINBOWS

RAINBOWS often appear in the sky in rainy weather, when the sun is quite low in the sky. They form because raindrops split up the light from the sun into a spread of different colors. This spread is called a spectrum. In science, white light can be split up into a colorful spectrum by shining it through a prism, or a wedge of glass. In this experiment a spectrum is produced by shining light through a wedge of water.

You will need: mirror, dish, reusable adhesive, pitcher of water, flashlight, piece of white cardboard.

Seven main colors can be seen in the rainbow. They are red (on the outside), orange, yellow, green, blue, indigo and violet (on the inside).

Split light into a rainbow

1 Lean the mirror against the side of the dish carefully. Secure it with reusable adhesive so that it slopes at an angle.

2 Pour water into the dish until it is 1-2 inches deep. This creates a wedge of water by the mirror.

3 Switch on the flashlight and shine the beam onto the water surface in front of the mirror. This should produce a spectrum, or rainbow.

FACT BOX

• White light is not really white. It is actually made up of light of many colors. They combine to make white.

• When light travels from air into water or glass (or back the other way), it bends. Some of the different colors in the light bend more than others. Blue light bends most, red light least. As a result, the colors start to separate out and the result is a spectrum – the colors of the rainbow.

This is what happens in a rainbow.

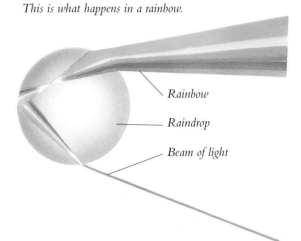

Rainbow

Raindrop

Beam of light

This is what happens in your experiment.

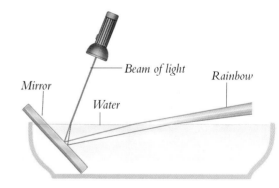

Mirror

Beam of light

Rainbow

Water

4   To look at your rainbow, hold up the white cardboard above the dish. You may need to alter the positions of the cardboard and flashlight before you can see it properly. It is also best if you do this part of the experiment in dim light.

THUNDER AND LIGHTNING

A thunderstorm is one of nature's greatest spectacles. Huge dark thunderclouds, as much as 6 miles deep, tower up through the sky. Meteorologists call them cumulonimbus. Lightning flashes zigzag between the clouds and fork down to the ground. The air is filled with cracks and rumbles of thunder, like the sound of guns in a battle. But what exactly are lightning and thunder? Lightning is a giant electric spark. Electricity builds up in thunderclouds as drops of water and lumps of ice whizz to and fro. Eventually, the electricity becomes so powerful that it jumps to other clouds or to the ground. The air in its path gets very hot and expands suddenly. This sets up a kind of explosion, which we hear as thunder.

Sieou-wen-ing sends bolts of lightning toward the earth. In Chinese mythology she is the mother of lightning.

Struck by lightning
A streak of lightning has struck this tree, leaving a trail of exposed wood on the bark.

Hail
Lumps of ice, called hailstones, often fall out of thunderclouds. Here, hailstones have covered a street in Pretoria, South Africa.

Flashes of lightning

A spectacular night display of lightning above distant mountains. Note that the lightning is not only traveling to earth, but is also jumping around between the clouds.

Lightning conductor

This church steeple has a lightning conductor. If lightning should strike, it will travel safely down the lightning conductor without causing damage to the rest of the building.

GAUGING THE RAIN

IN most parts of the world it rains on and off throughout the year. In some places more than several feet of rain can fall in a year. In others there is much less. How much rainfall do you get where you live? If it is very rainy, this project will keep you busy. Make this simple rain gauge and find out. Gauge is a name for a measuring instrument. If you live in a desert area, perhaps you had better pass on this experiment. You might have to wait for years to try out your rain gauge!

Don't forget your umbrella and rubber boots in the rain.

MATERIALS

You will need: scissors, tape, large jar (such as a candy jar), ruler, ballpoint pen, large plastic funnel, tall narrow jar or bottle, notebook.

Measure rainfall

1 Cut a length of tape that is the same height as the large jar and stick it on. Using the ruler, mark a scale on the tape at ½ inch intervals. Measure the diameter of the large jar and cut the funnel to exactly the same size.

2 Place the funnel in the jar, and your rain gauge is ready. Put the gauge outside, in an open space away from trees or shrubs. Look at your rain gauge at the same time each morning or evening to see if it has rained in the last 24 hours.

3 When it has rained, read on the scale how much water is in the jar. This is the rainfall for the past 24 hours. Make a note of the reading in your weather book. Remember to empty the jar before you return it to its place.

Being precise

You can measure the rainfall more accurately if you use a separate narrow measuring jar or bottle. First, stick another strip of tape along the side of this bottle. Pour water into the large collecting jar up to the ½-inch mark. Now pour this water into the measuring bottle. Mark ½ inch where the water level reaches. Divide the length from the bottom of the bottle to the ½-inch mark into ten equal parts. Each will be equivalent to .04 inch of rainfall. Extend the scale past the ½-inch mark to the top of the measuring bottle. Ask an adult to help you with this part of the experiment. You can use this bottle to measure the rainfall you collect, accurately to the nearest hundredth of an inch, just like professional meteorologists do.

Looking at rain

Some companies make all-in-one weather instruments, which are very handy when space is limited. With this particular instrument you can measure the temperature, amount of rainfall, wind direction and wind speed. This girl is reading the rain gauge on her all-in-one instrument.

FACT BOX

• The wettest place in the world is Mawsynram in India, where an average of nearly 40 feet of rain falls every year.

• New York and Sydney have a little over 40 inches of rain a year. Paris and London have about 24 inches a year.

• The driest place in the world is the Atacama Desert, west of the Andes in Chile, South America. Just a few showers of rain fall in parts of the desert every century.

• Sea storms can cause worse flooding than rainfall. Large waves form that can submerge coastal areas.

SNOW AND ICE

The beautiful shape of a snowflake, formed from delicate strands of ice. Snowflakes are among nature's greatest works of art. No two are exactly the same.

SNOW falls in winter in many countries. It also falls all year round in places near the north and south poles and at the top of high mountains. Snow is a form of precipitation that falls to the ground from the clouds. It forms at the tops of high clouds where the temperature is below freezing. Clusters of snowflakes fall from the clouds when they become heavy. But if the lower air is warm, they melt and fall as rain. Sometimes a mixture of snow and rain falls as sleet. A snowflake is a mass of tiny crystals of frozen water, or ice. If you look at a snowflake under a microscope, you will see that it has the shape of a six-pointed star. However, all snowflakes are different from one another. On many winter nights the ground becomes snow-white even when it has not been snowing. This white covering is frost. Frost forms when the ground gets cold and water vapor in the air condenses on it. The water immediately freezes into tiny sparkling crystals of ice.

Cover of snow
Thick snow has fallen in the Austrian alps. Snow falls all through the winter in the alps, the peaks of which rise to more than 15,000 feet.

Ice on glass
Look at the frost on a windowpane. The ice has formed feathery crystals where it froze.

Jack Frost
According to folk tales, Jack Frost makes the beautiful icy patterns you find outside on trees, plants and fences when the weather is freezing.

Chunks of ice
Most of the ice in the world is found in the ice caps at the north and south poles. Great chunks of ice are constantly breaking off and floating away as icebergs.

MASSES OF AIR

Air masses cross paths, and a storm may occur. After the storm, the dark clouds still hang overhead near Krissavik, Iceland.

GREAT bodies of air are moving through the atmosphere all the time. Each has a different temperature and contains a different amount of moisture. They are called air masses. While a single air mass is passing us by, the weather remains the same. But when another air mass comes along, the weather changes. When two air masses come up against each other, the weather almost always takes a turn for the worse. Thick clouds may form and storms break out at the boundary, or front, where the air masses meet. The weather settles down again after the front has passed by.

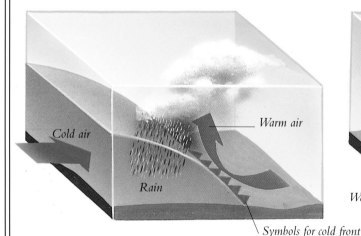

Cold front
Clouds form on a cold front as a wedge of cool air pushes underneath a mass of warm air. The warm air is forced to rise. As it cools, clouds form and rain falls.

Warm front
When a warm front moves in, the warm air rides up over the cold air and clouds will form. Usually rain falls as shown above.

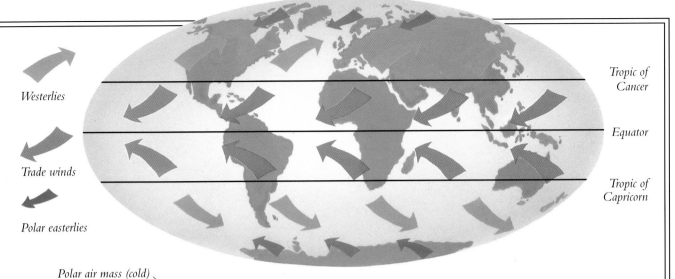

Westerlies

Trade winds

Polar easterlies

Tropic of Cancer

Equator

Tropic of Capricorn

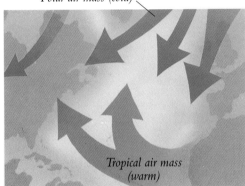

Polar air mass (cold)

Tropical air mass (warm)

World winds

This map shows the major air movements around the world, called wind belts. They are prevailing winds, which nearly always blow in the same direction. The trade winds are warm because they blow on either side of the equator. The westerlies are cool and blow north of the Tropic of Cancer and south of the Tropic of Capricorn. The polar easterlies are icy and blow around the north and south poles.

Polar fronts

Great masses of warm and cool air move around the earth. Warm air masses travel north and south away from the equator. Cold air masses travel south and north away from the north and south poles. They meet along boundaries called polar fronts.

Fast winds

On the open sea, sailing boats and ships have always relied on the trade winds and westerlies to speed them around the world.

HOLDING THE HEAT

Most climates vary around the world because different places receive different amounts of the sun's heat. However, other things affect the climate too. Places on seacoasts have a different climate from places inland. This is because land and water hold onto heat differently. Water takes longer to warm up and cool down than land. This means that summers are cooler and winters are milder on the coast than they are inland. Try this experiment with sand (land) and water (sea).

MATERIALS

You will need: pitcher of water, two bowls, sand, thermometer, notebook, pen, watch.

When you leave sand and water in the sunshine, you can feel how much hotter the sand becomes.

Measure temperature changes

1 Pour some water into one bowl and put some sand in the other. You do not need to measure them, but use roughly equal amounts.

2 Keep the bowls indoors and side by side in a cool place for a few hours. Then take their temperature. It should be the same.

3 Place the bowls side by side in the sunlight for an hour or two. Then take the temperature of the sand and water again.

Dark and light

In this experiment you will find that dark things and light things heat up and cool down differently. In hot countries, such as Saudi Arabia, they wear white robes to help keep cool because white things do not heat up as much as dark ones.

MATERIALS

You will need: two identical glass jars with lids (one painted black, one painted white), sand, spoon, thermometer, watch, notebook, pen.

1 Fill the two jars with sand to about the same level. Screw the lids on firmly. Place both jars outside in the sunshine, and leave them for two hours.

2 Now take the temperature of each jar. You should find that the sand in the black jar is hotter than the sand in the white jar.

3 Take the jars into the shade. Take the temperature of the sand in each one every 15 minutes. You should find that the sand in the black jar cools down faster than that in the white one. Dark objects warm up and cool down faster than pale ones.

4 Take the bowls indoors again to a cool place. Take their temperature every quarter of an hour. You will see that the sand cools down faster.

WORLD WEATHER

DIFFERENT parts of the world receive varying amounts of heat from the sun. This means different places have different climates. Places near the equator have the hottest climate. The climate gradually gets cooler as you move north and south away from the equator. The world can be divided into regions with similar kinds of climate. This is shown on the map. In tropical regions it is hot and wet. In dry desert regions it is usually hot, and scarcely any rain falls. In temperate regions it is not too hot and not too cold, and there is a reasonable amount of rainfall. Mountain regions have a climate that changes with height. In the polar climate, near the north and south poles, the weather is very cold almost all of the time.

This map shows the main kinds of climate found throughout the world. Different kinds of animals and plants live in each kind of climate.

Key to climates

Polar
Mountain
Cold forest
Temperate
Dry desert
Tropical

The cotton-top tamarin lives in the rainforests of Colombia in South America. It thrives in a hot, humid climate.

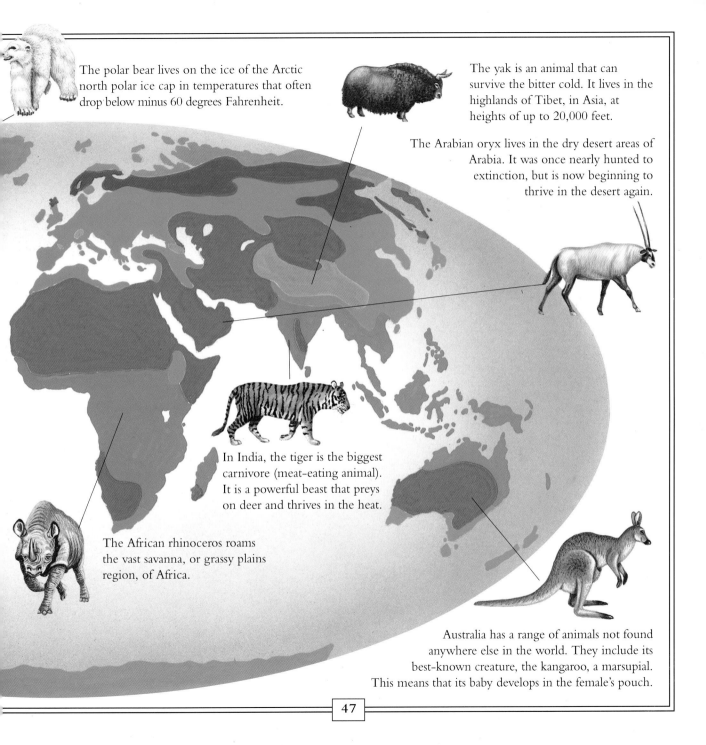

The polar bear lives on the ice of the Arctic north polar ice cap in temperatures that often drop below minus 60 degrees Fahrenheit.

The yak is an animal that can survive the bitter cold. It lives in the highlands of Tibet, in Asia, at heights of up to 20,000 feet.

The Arabian oryx lives in the dry desert areas of Arabia. It was once nearly hunted to extinction, but is now beginning to thrive in the desert again.

In India, the tiger is the biggest carnivore (meat-eating animal). It is a powerful beast that preys on deer and thrives in the heat.

The African rhinoceros roams the vast savanna, or grassy plains region, of Africa.

Australia has a range of animals not found anywhere else in the world. They include its best-known creature, the kangaroo, a marsupial. This means that its baby develops in the female's pouch.

WARM CLIMATES

This is one of the best-known desert plants found in southwestern USA. It is called the saguaro cactus, or the organ pipe cactus. Cacti are specially adapted to live in drought conditions, as they can store water.

In the desert
A Bedouin gazes across the greatest desert in the world, the Sahara in northern Africa. It covers an area that is nearly as big as the USA. Sahara is the Arabic word for desert. Most of the Sahara consists of hot sand dunes like you see in this picture. However, other areas are hard and rocky.

IN regions near the equator the climate stays hot all year round and plenty of rain falls. Due to this, plants grow quickly and keep growing all year long. Great forests flourish in these regions. They are called rainforests because of heavy rainfall. Thousands of different species, or kinds, of animals live there and can find plenty to eat all the time. On either side of the equatorial regions the climate stays hot and some areas become almost completely dry, forming deserts. In other parts, heavy rain may fall for only some of the year. This occurs in the African grasslands, known as the savanna. Even farther from the equator, there are regions with a temperate, or mild, warm climate. Most of Europe and the United States enjoy this kind of climate. Much of the world's most productive farmland is found in these regions.

Temperate plants

In temperate climates, trees such as beeches grow very well. They are deciduous, which means that they shed their leaves when it gets cold in the autumn.

Tropical plants

Trees grow and flower all through the year in the hot, damp tropical forests. Plant life in the forests grows rapidly, forming dense jungle.

African savanna

Scattered trees grow on the African savanna, where the climate is warm throughout the year. Rain falls only during the wet season; the rest of the year is dry.

Tropical animals

Alligators like the hot, moist climate of Florida. They love lazing in the sun, but can run as fast as you if they want to!

COOL CLIMATES

High in the mountains, the climate is always cool. The main kind of tree is the evergreen conifer. Conifers do not shed their leaves in the autumn. They keep them all through the year.

Hardy reindeer
Reindeer are among the hardiest of animals. They live in the cold, northern forests of the world and on the icy tundra of the Arctic. They grow heavy coats for the winter. Their hoofs are broad and flat to stop them from sinking too far into the snow. In winter they can survive by eating plants called lichens.

THE northern parts of North America, Europe and Asia have a cold, temperate climate. The winters are long and cold, and plenty of snow falls. The main plant life of this region is evergreen forest. It forms one of the two largest forest regions still remaining on earth. The tropical rainforests form the other big region. At the northern tips of North America, Europe and Asia it is too cold for trees to grow. These regions are called the tundra. In the tundra the winters are very long and harsh. Nevertheless, some plant life manages to survive, taking advantage of the few weeks of summer sun. North of the tundra, around the north pole, the ground is permanently covered with ice. Temperatures drop below minus 140 degrees Fahrenheit in the long, dark winters. At the other end of the earth the region around the south pole has a similarly severe climate.

Well-covered seal
Many kinds of seals live in the cold waters of the Arctic. Their bodies are covered with a thick layer of fatty blubber, which keeps out the cold.

Aquatic beaver
The beaver spends much of its time in the water too. It has a waterproof furry coat. It is found widely in the cool northern forests of North America.

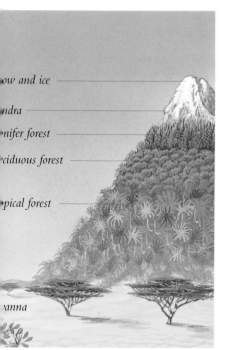

ow and ice
ndra
nifer forest
ciduous forest
pical forest
anna

Mount Kenya
A high mountain has several different climates on its slopes because the temperature falls the higher up you go. Here are the main kinds of climate found on Mount Kenya, which lies near the equator.

Sure-footed goat
A mountain goat straddles a rock cleft. It likes the cool temperatures of the mountains and is agile enough to clamber up the steepest slopes.

SEASONAL WEATHER

Ancient Britons built Stonehenge on Salisbury Plain as a means of marking the passing of the seasons.

IN most parts of the world, the day-to-day weather changes gradually throughout the year with the seasons. In the United States and Europe, which are in the northern hemisphere, it is cold in December (in the winter), warmer in March (spring), hot in June (summer) and cooler in September (autumn). The seasons are reversed in the southern hemisphere. The temperature changes with the seasons because of the way the earth is tilted in space as it travels around the sun. However, some parts of the world do not have these four seasons. For example, near the equator the weather stays hot and wet throughout the year. On the African savanna there are just two seasons – dry and wet.

North for the summer

In the summer, swallows in the northern hemisphere build their nests and raise their young.

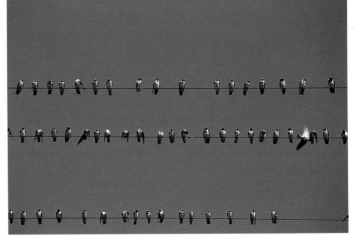

South for the winter

In the northern hemisphere's autumn, swallows gather on telephone lines and prepare to fly south for the winter.

Seasons

The seasons occur because of the way the earth spins as it circles in space around the sun. The axis of the earth is tilted at an angle to the direction it is traveling. This means that a particular place on earth is tilted toward and then away from the sun as the year passes. The more it is tilted toward the sun, the warmer it is. The more it is tilted away from the sun, the cooler it is.

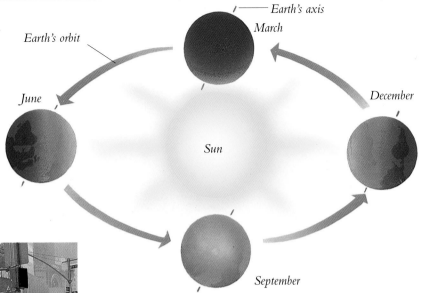

Earth's orbit

Earth's axis

March

June

December

Sun

September

Snowy December

A snowy scene in New York City, around Christmas time. It is near mid-winter. The temperature is only just above freezing, and there is a biting wind.

Sunny December

Many thousands of miles away in Australia, it is mid-summer and temperatures are hitting around 85 degrees Fahrenheit. Australia is in the southern hemisphere where the seasons are opposite to those in the northern hemisphere.

CHARGING UP

I N many parts of the world in summer, the weather can get very hot and sticky. Then we know that thunderstorms are likely to happen, producing lightning flashes and thunder.

Lightning happens when electricity builds up in the thunderclouds. It is a kind of electricity we call static electricity and is made up of tiny bits of electricity called electric charges. Lightning is produced when very high electric charges build up in clouds. We can build up tiny electrical charges using balloons.

Standing on end

If you comb your hair when it is very dry, you may make it electrically charged. You can make it stand on end and you may even hear crackling noises as tiny sparks fly around in your hair.

Make static electricity

1 Blow up a number of balloons and rub them against a sweater or something wool. Place the balloons in different places.

2 Put them on the ceiling, on the walls, on your friends! They stay because of electricity that does not move – static electricity.

You will need: balloons, balloon pump, hairbrush.

*You will need: plastic tablecloth,
tape, rubber gloves,
metal dish, fork.*

*Lightning zigzags
across the sky as
electric charges
build up in the
clouds and
jump around.*

Jumping electricity

In the last experiment, you built up tiny electrical
charges on the balloons by rubbing. The balloons
stuck to things because of the attraction of these
charges. Up in the clouds, high electrical charges
jump around. They create the flashes we call
lightning. You can make electricity jump with this
experiment.

1 Lay out the plastic cloth and tape
it to the table with the tape.
This prevents it from sliding around
and disrupting your experiment.

2 Wearing a rubber glove, slide the
dish back and forth over the
cloth for a few minutes. This will
charge it up with electricity.

3 With your ungloved hand, bring
the fork close to the dish and
you should see lightning, or a spark,
jump. It is easier to see in the dark.

THE CHANGING CLIMATE

THE weather in a region may change from day to day. But the climate, or the overall weather pattern, remains much the same. However, over long periods of time, the climate does change. Changes in the heat the sun gives out can make the earth hotter or colder. It causes ice ages, for example, when vast sheets of ice grow to cover large areas of the earth. Big meteorites can cause sudden changes in climate when they hit the earth and kick up huge amounts of dust into the atmosphere. This dust stops the sun's heat from reaching the ground, causing the temperature to fall steeply. Gradual changes are happening because of humans burning fuels. Burning releases more carbon dioxide gas into the atmosphere, turning it into a kind of greenhouse. This is slowly heating up our world by causing global warming.

A fireball streaks through the night sky. It is a lump of rock burning up as it plunges down to earth as a meteorite. Big meteorites can bring about a change in climate.

Global warming
If the world warms up enough, the ice at the north and south poles could melt. This will unlock vast amounts of water, which may cause the oceans to rise. Coastal cities like New York could be flooded or washed away.

Trees and climate
Scientists can study past changes in climate by measuring the width of the annual rings in tree trunks. Trees grow more when the climate is warmer.

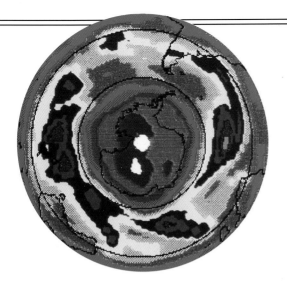

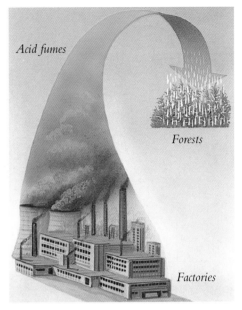

Acid rain

Acid fumes

Acid forms in the air when gases from cars and factory chimneys escape and combine with the tiny droplets of water in the clouds. Then when it rains, the rain is acid. Acid can be harmful to living things by scorching or burning them.

Forests

Factories

Ozone hole

In the 1980s, space scientists discovered a thinning of the ozone layer *(above)* in the atmosphere over Antarctica. This thinning, called an ozone hole, now happens regularly. If the ozone layer thins too much, it will let through rays from the sun that harm us.

FACT BOX
- About 65 million years ago, a huge meteorite crashed down on the earth and caused the climate to change. Many scientists believe that this killed off the dinosaurs and many other species, or kinds, of animals.

- The last ice age came to an end about 10,000 years ago. Geologists – the scientists who study the Earth – believe another ice age could happen in a few thousand years.

- Mexico City, in Central America, is sometimes so polluted that birds have been known to fall dead out of the skies. Most days the pollution blocks out the sun.

Dirty air

Fumes from traffic and factory chimneys affect the climate. This means that living things suffer when air quality changes. Sometimes cyclists have to wear masks where the air pollution is bad.

RECORDING THE WEATHER

Meteorologists do two main jobs. One is collecting information about what the weather is like now. The other is using this information to help them forecast what the weather is going to be like in the future. Meteorologists collect information about the weather at weather stations scattered around the world. They use a variety of measuring instruments. For example, thermometers measure the temperature, barometers measure the air pressure and hygrometers measure the humidity of the air. Wind vanes show the direction of the wind and anemometers measure wind speed. Meteorologists now also use space technology to help them. They send weather satellites into orbit to take pictures of clouds and measure temperatures and other weather conditions in the air. Satellites are useful as they can record weather in remote regions where there are no weather stations.

A rocket blasts off from Cape Canaverel in Florida, carrying a weather satellite called NOAA. It will circle the earth over the north and south poles and send cloud pictures back to earth, along with other weather data.

Weather balloon
Meteorologists are about to launch a weather balloon called a radio sonde. It carries instruments high into the atmosphere.

Measuring sunshine

This instrument is a sunshine recorder. The glass ball acts as a lens and, when the sun shines, it burns a piece of paper underneath. In this way the instrument records the length of time the sun is out.

Measuring wind

This small weather station has an anemometer (to measure the wind speed) and a wind vane mounted on poles above the roof. Note the wispy cirrus clouds in the sky.

Weather at sea

This is an automatic weather buoy. It carries a variety of instruments. Readings are transmitted automatically to weather stations or satellites passing overhead.

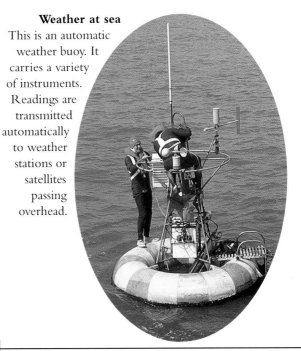

Measuring temperature

Here a meteorologist is reading the thermometers in a special enclosure called a Stevenson screen.

YOUR WEATHER STATION

YOU can set up your own weather station at home with a few simple instruments. You will be able to use some of the things we have shown you how to make earlier in the book, such as the weather vane, hygrometer and rain gauge. In addition, you will need a thermometer and a barometer, which can both be bought cheaply. Pick up some pine cones in the park and some seaweed at the beach.

Make a note
Take measurements with your weather instruments every day, and write them down in a notebook. Also, make a note of what the weather is like generally – clear, cloudy, rainy, frosty, and so on. Remember to make a note of the date!

Which way is the wind blowing?
Remember the arrow points in the direction from which the wind is blowing. A north wind blows from the north.

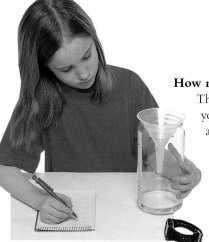

How humid is it?
Your hygrometer will help. Note the position of the pointer on the scale. When it tilts up, the air is moist and rain could be on the way.

How hot is it?
These thermometers at a weather station measure the temperature in the shade. Make sure you place your thermometer in the shade. It will then read the temperature of the air.

How much did it rain?
The rain gauge tells you this. Measure the amount of water in the jar. Use the measuring bottle to be accurate. Remember to empty the jar after you have finished.

These red clouds in the morning provide a warning of stormy weather to come.

No home weather station would be complete without pine cones. When they are ripe, pine cones open on dry days to shed their seeds. They close up if the weather is humid, or damp. Even after they have shed their seeds and fallen, pine cones still tend to open wider on dry days and close on damp days. Seaweed can also change as the humidity changes. If the weather is dry, the seaweed feels dry and brittle. If the weather is humid, the seaweed feels flexible and damp.

The puffy white cumulus clouds tell us the weather is going to stay fine.

Read the clouds

The kinds of clouds in the sky often give you a clue about how the weather is going to develop during the day.

FORECASTING

To help them prepare a weather forecast, meteorologists traditionally draw a number of weather charts, or maps. At certain times of the day, they gather all the latest information about the weather in their region and plot it on a chart, in the form of symbols. They then compare this chart with one they drew some hours before. This gives them an idea about how the weather is changing. Another chart is drawn that shows what they think the weather will be like in the near future. Using this, they issue a weather forecast. Meteorologists increasingly use computers to help them forecast. Computers can more easily trace patterns in past weather and show more accurately how the weather should develop in the future. However, you cannot always rely on these methods, as even the computers get it wrong sometimes!

Satellite weather
A weather satellite called GOES sent back this picture of North and South America.
It shows swirls of cloud scattered over the two continents and the oceans that surround them.

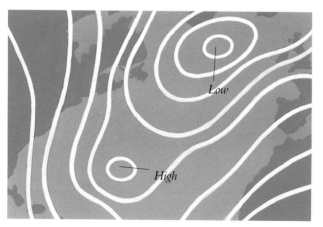

Low

High

The lines on this weather map of the Atlantic Ocean are called isobars. They connect areas with the same air pressure. Isobar means same pressure. Low shows the center of an area of low pressure. High shows the center of a high pressure area.

This map covers the British Isles and northern France. Again, the white lines are isobars.

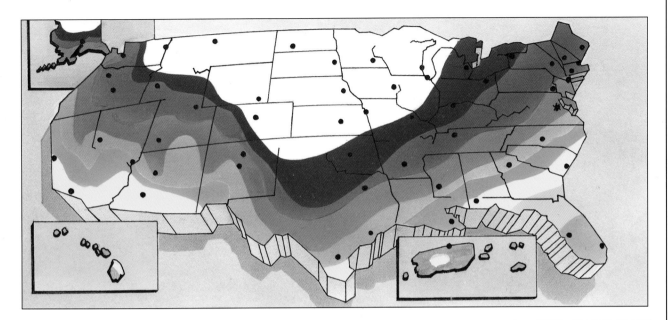

U.S.A weather

Newspapers often carry simplified weather maps such as this one, which shows the weather expected over the United States for a day in January. The different colors indicate different temperatures: white is coldest, orange is warmest.

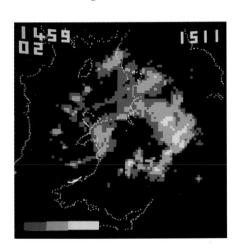

Radar scan

Meteorologists now use radar to detect rain. This weather radar scan shows showers taking place over North Wales in the United Kingdom. The yellow areas show the regions of heaviest rainfall.

FACT BOX

• Weather satellites can take pictures of the cloud cover over the earth at night as well as during the day.

• The World Meteorological Organization (WMO) is the main international organization connected with the weather. Weather forecasters send information about their local weather to the WMO. In return they can gain information about the weather in other parts of the world from the WMO.

• The chart weather forecasters prepare that shows the weather at a certain time is called a synoptic chart. The chart that shows what they think the weather will be at a certain time in the future is a prognostic chart.

INDEX

acid rain 57

air 10-15

  masses 42-3

  movement 20-1

  pressure 16-19, 58

Al Aziziyah 8

Alaska 11

alligators 16, 49

altocumulus 31

altostratus 31

anemometer 59

Altamont Pass 21

Antarctica 17, 57

atmosphere 10-15, 16, 42

Alps 40

Atacama Desert 39

Aurora 11

barometer 58, 60

Beaufort Scale 20-1

beaver 51

beeches 49

Bedouin 48

breezes 20-1

cacti 48

California 16, 17, 28

Cape Canaveral 58

carbon dioxide 12-13, 56

cirrocumulus 31

cirrostratus 31

cirrus 30, 31

climates 44-51, 56-7

clouds 10, 26-7, 30-3, 36, 40, 42, 58, 61

conifers 50-1

comets 11

conifers 50, 51

cotton-top tamarin 46

cumulonimbus 31

cumulus 30, 31

Death Valley 17

deserts 16, 38, 39, 46, 48

dew 32-3

dust devils 24

electric storms 36-7, 54-5

electricity 7, 54-5

Equator 7, 16, 46, 48, 52

Everglades 16

Florida 16, 25

forecasts, weather 4, 28, 58, 62-3

forests 50

fronts 42-3

    frost fairs 5

gales 20-1

global warming 56

goat 51

greenhouse effect 56

hail 36

Hawaii 33

Hemispheres 52-3

humidity 16, 26, 28-9, 33, 58, 60

hurricanes 20, 24-5

hygrometers 28-9, 58, 60

ice 5, 30, 36, 40-1

ice ages 5, 57

isobars 62

Jaipur 33

Joshua tree 16

kangaroo 47

land, temperature 21, 44

lightning 10, 36-7, 54-5

London 39

Majorca 32

Mawsynram 39

Mediterranean Sea 32

meteorologists 4, 22, 58-9, 62

meteorology 4, 22

meteors and meteorites 11, 56-7

Mexico City 57

migration 52

monsoons 33

Moon 10

Mount Kenya 51

Mount Tasman 27

mountainous regions 46, 50-1

New York 39, 53

nitrogen 12, 14

Northern Lights 11

oryx 47

oxygen 10, 12, 13, 14

ozone layer 10, 57

parachute 12

paragliding 12

pine cones 60-1

plants 13, 16, 33, 49, 50

polar bear 47

polar fronts 43

polar regions 7, 40, 41, 46-7, 50

pollution 57

precipitation 32, 40

pressure 16-19, 58

Pretoria 36

radar 63

radio sonde 58

rain 10, 26-7, 30, 32-3, 42, 57, 63

rain gauges 38-9, 60

rainbows 33-5

rainforests 16, 28, 48-9, 50

redwood trees 28

reindeer 50

rhinoceros 47

River Thames 5

Sahara 48

satellites 5, 58-9, 62-3

savanna 47, 48-9, 52

sea 21, 44, 59

seal 51

seasons 6, 52-3

seaweed 60-1

sky 12-13

snow 4, 10, 26-7, 40, 50, 53

solar power 7

solar prominences 7

Southern Lights 11

Space 10

spectrum 34-5

Stevenson screen 59

Stonehenge 52

storms 20, 24-5, 32, 36-7, 39, 42, 54-5, 61

stratus 31

stratocumulus 31

stratosphere 10, 11

Sun 5, 6-7, 27, 44-5, 53

sunlight 6-7, 10, 33, 59

sunshine recorder 59

sunspots 7

Sydney 39

swallows 52

temperate climate 46, 48-9

temperature 8-9, 16-17, 44-5, 59

thermo-strips 8

thermometers 8-9, 58, 60

thunder 10, 32, 36-7, 54-5

tiger 47

tornadoes 24-5

trees 16, 36, 49, 50

transpiration 29

tropical climate 46-9, 52

troposphere 10, 11

tundra 50

water cycle 26-9

water vapor 26-9

waterspouts 25

weather vanes 5, 22-3, 58, 60

whirlwinds 24

wind 5, 20-3, 43, 58-9

wind belts 43

wind power 21

yak 47

PICTURE CREDITS